Catterine A. K

C000046118

# THE HU

*Carpet*

# THE HUMBLE

## Carpet

Approaching the
Magnificence of Jesus

DOMINGOS AIOLFE

*I dedicate this book to Jesus, the source of inspiration and magnificence that permeates every page of this work. His divine presence is the guiding thread that leads us through the journey of humility, redemption and closeness with the Heavenly Father.*

*To the readers who embark on this journey, I hope that the message transmitted here is an invitation to become "humble carpets" in the face of God's greatness. May they experience the transformation and renewal that come from accepting our sinful condition and seeking purity in His divine love.*

*I would like to thank everyone who has been present along my path and who, in one way or another, contributed to making this project a reality. To my family and friends, whose support and encouragement were fundamental, my deepest gratitude.*

*May every page of this book serve as a reminder of the power of humility and the importance of seeking God's presence in our lives. May as we approach the Savior's sanctified feet, we find the true joy and transformation that only He can bring.*

**Title**

*"Draw close to God, and he will draw close to you." - James 4:8a*

*May this sacred word inspire us to incessantly seek divine closeness, making us humble rugs for the grandeur of our Creator.*

## Preface

*It is with great joy and humility that I present this book, "Humble Carpet - The Divine Proximity". From the moment the seed of this idea was planted in my heart, I felt the conviction that I needed to share this message with the world.*

*Throughout this writing journey, I delved into the depths of God's Word, seeking to understand the greatness of Jesus and the essence of divine holiness. With each step, I was impacted by the magnitude of love and mercy that overflow from the sacred pages.*

*The idea of the "humble rug" emerged as a powerful metaphor, showing us the way to divine closeness. I realized that as we humble ourselves before God, acknowledging our worthlessness and sinfulness, we are lifted into His presence and transformed by His divine touch.*

*Each chapter is a journey of reflection and discovery as we delve into Scripture, exploring the humility of heart that allows us to experience redemption and renewal in Christ. Through the search for purity, acceptance of our condition as sinners and total surrender to God, we are invited to live in full communion with Him.*

*I hope this book serves as a light that illuminates the path of those who yearn for a deeper experience with the Lord. May each word written here echo in the heart of the reader, inviting him to approach the sanctified feet of Jesus and find the true joy and peace that only He can provide.*

*I thank all those who have supported and encouraged me on this journey, especially my family and friends, whose love and prayers have been instrumental. I also thank God, the author of inspiration and the protagonist of each page of this book.*

*May the reading of this book be a blessing for every life that ventures into its pages. May the divine presence be a palpable reality in our lives, and may humility lead us to a transforming closeness with the Creator of the Universe.*

## Thanks

*At this special time, I want to express my deep gratitude to all the people who have contributed to the realization of this book. Every step of this journey was marked by the loving presence of God and the invaluable support of friends, family and colleagues.*

*First, I thank my Savior, Jesus Christ, for being my source of inspiration and motivation. His magnificence and divine closeness are at the heart of this work, and everything we have done has been with the aim of glorifying His name.*

*To my parents, my eternal thanks for their unconditional love, constant encouragement, and unwavering support. You always believed in me and encouraged me to pursue my dreams.*

*To my family, for sharing my passion for the Word of God and the Gospel, and for being my source of inspiration in every written word. Your support and understanding made this journey even more meaningful.*

*To my friends, who have been by my side through every challenge and achievement, thank you for reminding me of the importance of staying true to the message God has placed in my heart. Your friendship is a treasure that I value immensely.*

*To my mentors and colleagues, whose wise words and guidance guided me through the writing process, I am immensely grateful. Their contributions were fundamental to improve this work.*

*To readers, whose interest and support are a constant motivation to share the eternal truths found in the Scriptures. May this book reach your hearts and inspire you to seek divine closeness in your own lives.*

*I thank every person who prayed for me and for this project. Your prayers strengthened my faith and gave me the confidence I needed to carry on, even in the face of challenges.*

*Finally, I recognize that this book would not have been possible without God's grace and mercy. He is the principal author of this work, and it is my prayer that every word written here will be used for His purpose and glory.*

*May all praise go to Him, the Almighty, the Creator and Sustainer of all things. May His divine presence be the beacon that guides each reader to a life of humility, redemption, and closeness to the Heavenly Father.*

# SUMMARY

# CHAPTER 1

# THE DIVINE ENCOUNTER

*At the beginning of this spiritual journey, it is essential to understand the importance of the divine encounter. It is in this encounter that we can experience the magnificent presence of Jesus and be transformed by His grace. In this chapter, we will explore some biblical passages that highlight the nature of divine encounter and its impact on our lives.*

**The Call to Search:**

"He who dwells in the shelter of the Most High shall rest in the shadow of the Almighty" (Psalm 91:1).

Since ancient times, God has called His people to seek Him and find refuge in His presence. Psalm 91 invites us to dwell in the shelter of the Most High, to take refuge under His shadow. This is a call to approach God, seeking a personal encounter with Him.

**The Promise of Search and Encounter**

"Ye shall seek me, and find me, when ye seek me with all your heart" (Jeremiah 29:13).

God promises that when we seek Him with all our hearts, we will find Him. He longs for an intimate relationship with us and invites us to sincerely and committedly seek His presence. This divine encounter is not reserved for just a privileged few, but for all those who sincerely seek Him.

**Approaching Jesus**

"Draw near to God, and he will draw near to you!" (James 4:8a, New Living Translation).

James encourages us to draw close to God, promising that He will also draw close to us. This invitation reminds us that God is always ready to meet us, but it is necessary that we take the initiative to approach Him with an open and thirsty heart.

**The Transformation in the Encounter**

"But we all, with unveiled face, reflecting as a mirror the glory of the Lord, are being transformed into the same image from glory to glory, as by the Spirit of the Lord" (2 Corinthians 3:18).

When we meet Jesus, we are transformed. This transformation is not just an external change, but a change of heart and character. As we yield ourselves to His presence and allow His Spirit to work in us, we are molded into the image of Christ and reflect His glory.

**Meeting in the Secret Places**

"But you, when you pray, go into your room, and when you have shut your door, pray to your Father who is in secret, and your Father who sees in secret will reward you" (Matthew 6:6).

Jesus teaches us about the importance of meeting God personally in secret places, where we can pray and seek His face without distractions. These moments of intimacy are essential for strengthening our relationship with Him and experiencing His presence in a profound way.

## The Communion Encounter

"For where two or three are gathered in my name, there am I in their midst" (Matthew 18:20).

When we come together as the body of Christ, in fellowship and worship, we experience the powerful presence of Jesus. He promises to be in the midst of those who gather in His name, strengthening and encouraging their faith.

## The Desire to Know Christ

"Yea, indeed, I count all things loss for the surpassing worth of knowing Christ Jesus my Lord, for whose sake I have lost all things, and count them as refuse, that I might gain Christ" (Philippians 3:8).

The apostle Paul expresses his deep desire to know Christ above all things. He recognizes that there is nothing more valuable than a relationship with Jesus and that all other achievements and accomplishments pale in comparison to the knowledge of Christ.

# CHAPTER 2

# RECOGNIZING THE GREATNESS OF JESUS

*In this chapter, we will delve into the theme of the greatness of Jesus. Through biblical passages, we will examine who He is and how His greatness is revealed in Scripture. As we recognize His greatness, we are invited to worship Him, surrender to Him, and seek a deeper relationship with our Lord.*

## The Only Begotten Son of God

"For God so loved the world that he gave his only begotten Son, that whoever believes in him should not perish but have eternal life" (John 3:16).

This passage is one of the best known verses in the Bible and reveals to us the greatness of God's love in sending His Only Begotten Son, Jesus Christ, to save mankind. Jesus is God's supreme gift to humanity, demonstrating His greatness as the beloved Son who came into the world to reconcile us with the Father.

## The Name upon Every Name

"Therefore God exalted him to the highest place and gave him the name that is above every name, so that at the name of Jesus every knee should bow, in heaven and on earth and under the earth" (Philippians 2:9-10).

These verses emphasize Jesus' exaltation by God the Father and the greatness of His name. The name of Jesus is above every name and has complete authority over everything in heaven, on earth and under the earth. Recognizing the greatness of Jesus means recognizing the supremacy and sovereignty that He possesses.

**The Creator and Sustainer of All Things**

"For by him all things were created, in heaven and on earth, visible and invisible, whether thrones or dominions, powers or authorities; all things were created through him and for him. He is before all things, and in him all things hold together" (Colossians 1:16-17).

These verses highlight the greatness of Jesus as the Creator of all things. Not only did he bring the visible universe into being, but he is also the

9

sustainer of all that exists. All creation, visible and invisible, was made by Him and for Him. This demonstrates His authority and power as the supreme Lord over all things.

**The Incarnate Word**

"In the beginning was the Word, and the Word was with God, and the Word was God... And the Word was made flesh, and dwelt among us, full of grace and truth; and we beheld his glory, the glory as of the only begotten of the Father" (John 1:1,14).

This passage from the Gospel of John reveals the greatness of Jesus as the Incarnate Word, the very God who became flesh and dwelt among us. He is eternal and divine, equal to the Father, and He chose to humble Himself by taking human form to save us. Recognizing His greatness means understanding the majesty and divinity He possessed before coming to earth.

## The Lamb of God

"The next day John saw Jesus coming towards him, and he said, Behold, the Lamb of God, who takes away the sin of the world!" (John 1:29).

This statement by John the Baptist reveals the greatness of Jesus as the Lamb of God, the perfect sacrifice that takes away the sin of the world. He is the fulfillment of Old Testament prophecies, the promised Savior who brings redemption and reconciliation with God. By recognizing His greatness as the Lamb of God, we are invited to receive forgiveness and salvation through Him.

**The Promised Messiah**

"And she shall bear a son, and thou shalt call his name Jesus, for he shall save his people from their sins" (Matthew 1:21).

These words of the angel to Joseph reveal the greatness of Jesus as the promised Messiah. He came into the world to fulfill Old Testament prophecies and to save His people from their sins. As we recognize His greatness as the Messiah, we are invited to place our faith and trust in Him as our Savior.

**The High Priest**

"Therefore, since we have a great high priest who has passed into heaven, Jesus the Son of God, let us hold firmly to the faith we profess" (Hebrews 4:14).

Jesus is revealed as our great high priest, who intercedes for us before God. He entered heaven and is at the right hand of the Father, interceding for us continually. His greatness as our High Priest assures us that we have direct access to God and that He represents us before the Father.

# CHAPTER 3

# THE ESSENCE OF HOLINESS

*In this chapter, we'll delve into the essence of holiness, exploring the biblical meaning of this divine attribute and its importance in our lives as followers of Jesus Christ. Through various passages in the Bible, we will examine what holiness represents, how holy God is, and how we are called to pursue a life of holiness in communion with Him.*

## The Definition of Holiness

"Be holy, for I am holy" (1 Peter 1:16).

These words of God, recorded by the Apostle Peter, concisely summarize the essence of holiness. To be holy means to be set apart, dedicated, and consecrated to God. It is a call to live in accordance with nature and divine standards, reflecting God's purity and morality in our lives.

## The Holiness of God

"Who is like you, O Lord, among the gods? Who is like you, glorious in holiness, terrible in glorious deeds, working wonders?" (Exodus 15:11).

God's holiness is one of the attributes most emphasized in Scripture. He is totally separate from sin and evil, perfect in His purity and righteousness. His holiness is matchless and incomparable, and His glory is manifested through His wonderful works. As we recognize God's holiness, we are moved to a deep reverence and a desire to draw closer to Him.

## The Call to Holiness

"Therefore, sanctify yourselves and be holy, for I am the Lord your God. Keep my statutes and do them. I am the Lord who sanctifies you" (Leviticus 20:7-8).

God calls His people to be holy even as He is holy. This call to holiness is an invitation to separate from sin and worldly practices and to consecrate ourselves to Him. Holiness is not optional, but an expression of our relationship with God. It is through sanctification that we become more like Him.

## Holiness as a Distinctive

"But as he who called you is holy, so be holy in all your conduct, for it is written, 'Be holy, because I am holy'" (1 Peter 1:15-16).

Holiness is a differentiator for followers of Jesus Christ. It distinguishes us from the world and testifies to our identity as children of God. The way we live should reflect God's holiness and His work in us. Holiness is not just a position but also a daily practice that shapes every area of our lives.

## The Standard of Holiness

"Therefore the Lord himself will give you a sign: Behold, a virgin shall conceive and bear a son, and shall call his name Emmanuel" (Isaiah 7:14).

In the Old Testament, the prophet Isaiah prophesied of the birth of Jesus, the promised

Messiah. Jesus the Emmanuel embodies the ultimate standard of holiness. He lived a perfect, sinless life, and His example challenges us to seek holiness in our own lives. He is the supreme model of holiness that we should follow.

**The Holiness and Grace of God**

"For by grace are ye saved through faith; and that not of yourselves: it is the gift of God" (Ephesians 2:8).

Holiness cannot be achieved by our own efforts. We are sinners and incapable of becoming holy on our own. However, it is by God's grace that we are saved and enabled to live a holy life. It is through faith in Jesus Christ and the work of the Holy Spirit in us that we are transformed and empowered to pursue holiness.

## Holiness as a Continuous Quest

"Pursue peace with all men, and holiness, without which no one will see the Lord" (Hebrews 12:14).

The pursuit of holiness is an ongoing process in our lives as followers of Jesus. We should seek to live in peace with all and actively pursue sanctification. This requires a daily commitment to deny sin, pursue holiness through the Word of God, the power of the Holy Spirit, and fellowship with fellow believers.

# CHAPTER 4

# THE CALL TO HUMILITY

*In this chapter, we will explore the theme of the call to humility. The Bible teaches us about the importance and value of humility before God and others. Through several biblical passages, we will examine what it means to be humble, how Jesus is the supreme example of humility and how we can cultivate this virtue in our lives.*

**The Definition of Humility**

"Clothe yourselves with humility, for God resists the proud, but gives grace to the humble" (1 Peter 5:5b).

Humility is a virtue that reflects an attitude of submission, modesty and recognition of our dependence on God. It is the opposite of arrogance and pride. By covering ourselves with humility, we make room for God's grace to act in our lives.

**The Supreme Example of Humility - Jesus**

"Take my yoke upon you and learn from me, for I am gentle and humble in heart, and you will find rest for your souls" (Matthew 11:29).

Jesus is the supreme example of humility. He stripped Himself of His divine glory to become a servant, demonstrating humility in all His actions and words. He invites us to learn from Him and adopt His posture of meekness and humility. By following Jesus' example, we find rest for our souls and experience the fullness of His grace.

## The Exaltation of Humility

"Humble yourselves, therefore, under the mighty hand of God, that he may lift you up in due time" (1 Peter 5:6).

Humility is not a sign of weakness, but an attitude that God values. He promises to exalt those who humble themselves before Him. God's exaltation is not based on our seeking personal recognition, but on our willingness to submit to His will and trust in His sovereignty.

## The Call to Servitude

"Whoever wants to be first, let him be the last and the one who serves all" (Mark 9:35).

Jesus calls us to adopt an attitude of service and humility. He teaches that true greatness is not in seeking high places, but in serving others with love and selflessness. By placing ourselves in the position of servants, following the example of Jesus, we reveal humility in our actions.

## Humility towards God

"He has shown you, O man, what is good and what the Lord requires: do justice, love faithfulness, and walk humbly with your God" (Micah 6:8).

The prophet Micah reminds us of the importance of walking humbly with God. This involves submission to His will, doing justice, and loving faithfulness. Humility leads us to recognize that God is our Creator and Lord, and that we depend completely on Him in all areas of our lives.

## Humility towards Others

"First of all, however, put on love, which is the perfect link. Let the peace of Christ be the judge in your hearts, since you were called to live in peace, as members of one body. And be thankful" (Colossians 3:14-15).

Humility is also expressed in our relationships with others. We are called to clothe ourselves in love and seek peace. Humility leads us to value others, recognize their needs, and seek unity in the body of Christ. Gratitude is also a fruit of humility, as we recognize that everything we have comes from God.

## Humility and the Grace of God

"But he gives greater grace. Therefore he says, 'God resists the proud, but gives grace to the humble.' Submit yourselves therefore to God; but resist the devil, and he will flee from you" (James 4:6-7).

Humility puts us in a position of dependence and submission to God. When we humble ourselves before Him, He bestows His abundant grace upon us. This grace enables us to resist the devil and overcome the temptations that surround us. Humility is a way to experience God's provision and power in our lives.

# CHAPTER 5

# CONSCIOUSNESS OF OUR INSIGNIFICANCE

*In this chapter, we will explore the theme of awareness of our insignificance before God. The Bible teaches us about the greatness of God and our limitation as human beings. Through several biblical passages, we will examine how we can develop a healthy awareness of our insignificance and how this leads us to a deep dependence and reverence for God.*

## The Greatness of God

"O Lord, our Lord, how excellent is Your name in all the earth! For You have set forth Your majesty in the heavens" (Psalm 8:1).

These verses from Psalm 8 highlight the greatness and majesty of God. He is the Creator of all things and His glory is manifested throughout the earth. Recognizing God's greatness helps us understand our insignificance compared to Him.

## The Human Limitation

"What is man, that You are mindful of him? And the son of man, that You care for him? Yet You have made him a little lower than the angels, and You have crowned him with glory and honor" (Psalm 8:4-5).

These verses from Psalm 8 also reveal our limitedness as human beings compared to the greatness of God. Although we are created in God's image and crowned with glory and honor, we are insignificant compared to His majesty. This leads us to a healthy awareness of our own smallness.

**The Wisdom of God**

"O the depth of the riches both of the wisdom and knowledge of God! How unsearchable are his judgments, and how inscrutable are his ways!" (Romans 11:33).

Paul, in the letter to the Romans, extols the unfathomable wisdom and knowledge of God. Our awareness of our insignificance is deepened when we recognize the immensity of divine wisdom. We cannot fully understand God's ways, but we can trust in His sovereignty and depend on Him.

## The Fall of Humanity

"For all have sinned and fall short of the glory of God" (Romans 3:23).

The awareness of our insignificance is also strengthened by the reality of our sinful condition. The Bible teaches us that all have sinned and fallen short of the glory of God. We are unable to reach perfection on our own and are dependent on God's grace for our salvation.

## The Humility of John the Baptist

"I am not the Christ, but I am sent before him. He who has the bride is the bridegroom; but the friend of the bridegroom, who stands by and hears him, rejoices greatly at the voice of the bridegroom. So then this joy of mine is fulfilled. He must increase, and I must decrease" (John 3:28-30).

John the Baptist is an example of humility and awareness of his insignificance before Jesus. He recognized that his function was to prepare the way for the Messiah, and he did not consider himself worthy even to untie Jesus' sandals. This humble attitude, aware of our own smallness, teaches us to put God first and to diminish while He grows in our lives.

**The Call to Addiction**

"Seek the Lord while he may be found, call upon him while he is near" (Isaiah 55:6).

The awareness of our insignificance leads us to seek and depend on God. The prophet Isaiah exhorts us to seek the Lord while He may be found and to call upon Him while He is near.

30

Recognizing our limitations and smallness, we are led to trust and depend completely on God in all areas of our lives.

**God's Sufficient Grace**

"But he said to me, My grace is sufficient for you, for my power is made perfect in weakness. Therefore I will boast all the more gladly in my weaknesses, that the power of Christ may rest in me" (2 Corinthians 12:9).

When we become aware of our insignificance, we also recognize the sufficiency of God's grace in our lives. Paul, in his letter to the Corinthians, declares that the grace of God is sufficient for us. In our weaknesses, God's strength is manifested. This awareness leads us to trust in His grace and depend completely on Him.

# CHAPTER 6

# ACCEPTANCE OF OUR CONDITION AS SINNERS

*In this chapter, we will delve into the theme of accepting our condition as sinners. The Bible teaches us about the reality of sin in our lives and the need to recognize our fallen condition. Through various biblical passages, we will examine the truth about sin, the need for acceptance and how it leads to repentance and seeking God.*

## The Fall of Humanity

"Therefore, just as sin entered the world through one man, and death through sin, and so death spread to all men, because all sinned" (Romans 5:12).

These verses highlight the reality of the fall of mankind through the sin of Adam and Eve. Since then, we all share in this fallen condition and inherit the tendency to sin. Recognizing our condition as sinners is the first step towards accepting our need for salvation.

## The Consciousness of Sin

"As for me, I know that nothing good dwells in me, that is, in my flesh. For I have the desire to do what is good, but I am unable to carry it out" (Romans 7:18).

The apostle Paul expresses his awareness of sin in his own life. He recognizes that there is nothing good in his human nature and that he struggles with his own sinful inclinations. This awareness of sin leads us to accept our fallen condition and seek a solution to this situation.

**The Truth About Sin**

"If we say that we have no sin, we deceive ourselves, and the truth is not in us. If we confess our sins, he is faithful and just to forgive us our sins and to cleanse us from all unrighteousness" (1 John 1:8-9).

John, in his first letter, reminds us of the undeniable truth that we all sin. To deny our status as sinners is to deceive ourselves. However, when we recognize our sins and confess them to God, He is faithful to forgive and cleanse us. Acceptance of our sinful condition opens the way to forgiveness and restoration in Christ.

## God's Search for Sinners

"For the Son of Man came to seek and to save what was lost" (Luke 19:10).

These words of Jesus reveal His mission to seek and save those who are lost in their sins. He came to rescue sinners and offer salvation. When we accept our condition as sinners, we open ourselves to receive God's love and grace through Jesus Christ.

## The Call to Repentance

"Repent ye therefore, and be converted, that your sins may be blotted out" (Acts 3:19).

Repentance is essential in accepting our condition as sinners. We must turn to God, acknowledging our sins and turning away from them. Genuine repentance leads to a transformation of heart and opens us to reconciliation with God.

## God's Redeeming Grace

"But God demonstrates his own love for us in that while we were still sinners, Christ died for us" (Romans 5:8).

Accepting our condition as sinners leads us to understand and value God's immense love for us. While we were still sinners, Christ died for us on the cross. It is through His death and resurrection that we receive redemption and forgiveness of our sins. God's grace abounds and is freely offered to us when we accept our sinful condition and trust Christ as our Savior.

## The Pursuit of Sanctification

"Or do you not know that the unrighteous will not inherit the kingdom of God? Be not deceived: neither fornicators, nor idolaters, nor adulterers, nor effeminate men, nor sodomites, nor thieves, nor covetous, nor drunkards, nor cursed

beings, nor thieves, will inherit the kingdom of God. And such were some of you; But you were washed, but you were sanctified, but you were justified in the name of the Lord Jesus Christ and in the Spirit of our God" (1 Corinthians 6:9-11).

These verses from Paul to the Corinthians emphasize that although we were sinners, we were washed, sanctified and justified in Christ. Acceptance of our sinful condition is not an end in itself, but the beginning of a journey of sanctification. We are called to turn from our sinful lifestyles and live up to God's standards.

# CHAPTER 7

# DRAWING CLOSE TO THE PRESENCE OF JESUS

*In this chapter, we will delve into the topic of drawing closer to the presence of Jesus. The Bible teaches us about the importance and necessity of drawing close to Him, seeking deeper intimacy and relationship. Through various biblical passages, we will examine how we can approach the presence of Jesus, the benefits of this closeness and how to cultivate a life of communion with Him.*

**A Promise of Jesus**

"I am the way, the truth and the life. No one comes to the Father except through me" (John 14:6).

Jesus clearly stated that He is the way to approach God. He is the truth that reveals the character and will of God, and it is through Him that we find eternal life. Recognizing this truth propels us to seek and approach the presence of Jesus.

**The Quest for the Presence of Jesus**

"You will seek me and find me when you seek me with all your heart" (Jeremiah 29:13).

God promises that if we seek Him with all our hearts, we will find Him. Approaching the presence of Jesus requires a sincere and committed search. It is a deep longing that drives us to dedicate time and effort to knowing and being with Him.

**Approaching with Confidence**

"Let us therefore come boldly to the throne of grace, that we may obtain mercy and find grace to help us in our time of need" (Hebrews 4:16).

Coming into the presence of Jesus involves trust in His grace and mercy. We can boldly come to Him, knowing that He is ready to receive us and help us with all our needs. That confidence encourages us to seek deeper fellowship with Him.

**The Importance of Prayer**

"Pray without ceasing" (1 Thessalonians 5:17).

Prayer is a means by which we approach the presence of Jesus. It is through communication with Him that we establish a personal and intimate

41

dialogue. Prayer allows us to express our wants, needs and praise to God, strengthening our connection with Him.

## The Word of God as a Path to the Presence of Jesus

"You search the Scriptures, because in them you think you have eternal life, and they are they which testify of me" (John 5:39).

The Word of God reveals to us the person and will of Jesus. Through reading, studying, and meditating on the Scriptures, we come closer to the presence of Jesus as they testify of Him. The Bible is a guide to knowing and relating to Him in a deeper way.

**Worship as a Path to the Presence of Jesus**

"But the hour is coming, and now is, when true worshipers will worship the Father in spirit and truth, for the Father seeks such to worship Him" (John 4:23).

Worship is a means by which we approach the presence of Jesus. When we worship God in spirit and in truth, He reveals Himself to us in a special way. Worship connects us with the heart of God and involves us in an intimate relationship with Him.

**The Power of the Holy Spirit in Approaching Jesus**

"But when he, the Spirit of truth, comes, he will guide you into all the truth; for he will not speak on his own, but whatever he hears he will speak, and he will declare to you what is to come" (John 16:13).

The Holy Spirit is sent by Jesus to guide us into all truth. He enables us to approach the presence of Jesus, revealing His will to us and teaching us about Him. The power of the Holy Spirit helps us to have a deep and meaningful fellowship with Jesus.

# CHAPTER 8

# THE CARPET METAPHOR

*In this chapter, we will explore the rug metaphor in relation to our position before Jesus. The rug metaphor helps us understand humility, submission and total surrender of ourselves to Him. Through various biblical passages, we will examine the importance of this metaphor, how it applies to our lives, and what it means to be a rug for Jesus.*

## The Carpet Metaphor

The carpet metaphor refers to the idea of being humble and submissive before Jesus, allowing Him to pass over us and His holy feet not to touch the ground. This metaphor illustrates our condition as sinners and the greatness and holiness of Jesus. By becoming a mat for Him, we recognize our insignificance and dependence on Him.

## Humility and Submission

"Clothe yourselves with humility, for God resists the proud, but gives grace to the humble" (1 Peter 5:5b).

The carpet metaphor leads us to a deep humility and submission before God. Peter exhorts us to put on humility, recognizing that God resists the proud but gives grace to the humble. Being a mat for

Jesus implies emptying ourselves, abandoning pride and arrogance.

## The Holiness of Jesus

"Holy, holy, holy is the Lord of hosts; the whole earth is full of his glory!" (Isaiah 6:3).

The carpet metaphor highlights the holiness of Jesus. Just as Isaiah testified to God's holiness, we acknowledge that Jesus is holy and worthy of all reverence and worship. By being a rug for Him, we recognize His greatness and our insignificance before Him.

## Jesus' Addiction

"I am the vine, you are the branches. He who abides in me, and I in him, the same bears much fruit; for without me you can do nothing" (John 15:5).

The carpet metaphor leads us to a deep dependence on Jesus. He is the vine and we are the branches. Without Him, we can do nothing. By surrendering and becoming a rug for Him, we recognize that our strength, wisdom, and abilities come from Him.

**The Call to Servitude**

"Whoever wants to be first, let him be the last and the one who serves all" (Mark 9:35).

Jesus calls us to adopt an attitude of service and humility. He teaches that true greatness is not in seeking high places, but in serving others with love and selflessness. Being a rug for Jesus means putting the interests of others above our own and being willing to serve in humility.

**The Renunciation of Self**

"Then Jesus said to his disciples, If anyone wants to come after me, let him deny himself and take up his cross and follow me" (Matthew 16:24).

The rug metaphor also involves self-denial. Jesus calls us to deny ourselves, to take up our cross and follow Him. This implies abandoning our own desires and interests, putting Jesus first. Being a rug for Him means being willing to give up our selfishness and submit our will to God's will.

## The Example of Jesus

"For the Son of Man did not come to be served, but to serve, and to give his life as a ransom for many" (Mark 10:45).

The carpet metaphor finds its supreme example in Jesus. He came into the world not to be served, but to serve and to give His life as a ransom for many.

By becoming a rug for Him, we follow His example of service

**CHAPTER 9**

# SUBMISSION TO THE DIVINE PURPOSE

*In this chapter, we will explore the subject of submission to divine purpose. The Bible teaches us about the importance of surrendering to God's will and submitting to His plan for our lives. Through various biblical passages, we will examine what submission means, how we can discern divine purpose, and how we can live in alignment with it.*

## God's will

"Do not get drunk with wine, in which there is dissolution, but be filled with the Spirit, speaking to one another in psalms, singing and making melody in your heart to the Lord, in hymns and spiritual songs, giving thanks always for everything to God and the Father in the name of our Lord Jesus Christ" (Ephesians 5:18-20).

God's will for us, first and foremost, is to be filled with the Holy Spirit. When we are filled with the Spirit, we are empowered to discern and submit to God's will in all areas of our lives. This involves a life of praise, gratitude and constant search for God's presence.

**Submission to God**

"Commit your way to the Lord; trust in him, and he will do it" (Psalm 37:5).

To submit to God means to completely surrender our way to Him. It means trusting that He has the best plan for us and that He will take care of all our needs. Submission to God involves an attitude of surrender, trust, and obedience to His will.

## The Quest for the Kingdom of God

"But seek first his kingdom and his righteousness, and all these things shall be added to you" (Matthew 6:33).

Seeking God's kingdom means putting Him first in our lives. It involves prioritizing His government and His will above our own desires and ambitions. When we submit to the divine purpose, all other necessary things will be added to us.

## The Renewal of the Mind

"Do not be conformed to this world, but be transformed by the renewing of your mind, so that you may prove what is the good, acceptable and perfect will of God" (Romans 12:2).

Submission to the divine purpose requires a renewing of the mind. We need to abandon the world's standards and values and adopt the mind of Christ. This happens through studying and meditating on God's Word, allowing God's truth to transform our thoughts and perspectives.

## The Example of Jesus

"In everything, be submissive to your earthly masters, not only the good and humble, but also the wicked. For it is merit before God if, for conscience' sake, one bears afflictions suffering unjustly. that they should follow in his steps" (1 Peter 2:18-21).

Jesus is the ultimate example of submission to divine purpose. He suffered unjustly, but endured it patiently for our sakes. In following in the footsteps of Jesus, we are called to endure adversity and hardship in obedience to God. Submission to the divine purpose requires faith, perseverance, and imitating the example of Christ.

## The Role of the Holy Spirit

"But when he, the Spirit of truth, comes, he will guide you into all the truth; for he will not speak on his own authority, but whatever he hears he will speak, and he will declare to you what is to come" (John 16:13).

The Holy Spirit is sent by God to guide us and enable us to live in alignment with divine purpose.

He will lead us into the truth and reveal to us the will of God in every aspect of our lives. We need to depend on the Holy Spirit and be sensitive to His leading to live in submission to the divine purpose.

## The Joy of Submission

"For in me I have great contentment and hope, and I know that for your sakes I will remain and continue with you all, for your progress and joy in the faith" (Philippians 1:25).

Submission to divine purpose brings joy and contentment in our journey of faith. When we surrender to God's will, we experience His care, direction, and blessing in our lives. Joy is not only in the fulfillment of the divine purpose, but also in the very process of submission and trust in God.

# CHAPTER 10

# THE SEARCH FOR PURITY

*In this chapter, we will explore the theme of the quest for purity. The Bible teaches us about the importance of living a pure and holy life before God. Through various biblical passages, we will examine the meaning of purity, the benefits of this pursuit and how we can cultivate a life of purity in all areas of our existence.*

## .The Call to Holiness

"But as He who called you is holy, so be holy in all your conduct" (1 Peter 1:15).

God calls us to holiness, to the pursuit of purity in all areas of our lives. He is holy and wants us to be holy too. Purity is not just an outward action, but a way of life that reflects God's holiness.

## The Purity of the Heart

"Blessed are the pure in heart, for they shall see God" (Matthew 5:8).

Purity begins in the heart. To be pure in heart means to have an upright motive and intent, free from selfishness and impurities. Those who are pure in heart are promised to see God and experience deeper fellowship with Him.

## To Sexual Purity

"Flee from impurity. Any other sin that a person commits is outside the body; but he who practices immorality sins against his own body" (1 Corinthians 6:18).

Sexual purity is an important aspect of the pursuit of purity. God calls us to flee sexual impurity and keep our sexuality within the limits set by Him. This involves abstinence before marriage and fidelity in marriage. Sexual purity not only honors God, but also promotes healthy relationships and the preservation of intimacy for the proper context.

## The Purity of Thoughts

"Finally, brothers, whatever is true, whatever is noble, whatever is right, whatever is pure, whatever is lovely, whatever is of good repute, if there is any excellence and if there is anything worthy of praise, dwell on these things" (Philippians 4:8).

Purity of thought is essential to the pursuit of purity. We must discipline our minds to think of things that are true, noble, just, pure, and praiseworthy. This involves rejecting impure, negative, and sinful thoughts and filling our minds with thoughts that please God.

**Purity in Words**

"Let no unwholesome talk proceed out of your mouths, but only what is good for edification, that it may minister grace to those who hear" (Ephesians 4:29).

Purity also extends to our words. We should avoid speaking impure, vulgar, or offensive words. Instead, our words should be uplifting, graceful, and able to bless others. Purity in words reflects a pure heart and brings life and encouragement to those who hear us.

## Purity in Relationships

"For this reason a man shall leave his father and mother and be joined to his wife, and the two shall become one flesh" (Ephesians 5:31).

Purity in relationships involves faithfulness and mutual respect. God established the marriage union as a symbol of unity and purity. We must cultivate healthy relationships based on love, respect and fidelity, avoiding any form of infidelity, deceit or impurity.

## Purity as a Process

"But we all, with unveiled face, reflecting as a mirror the glory of the Lord, are being transformed into the same image from glory to glory, as by the Spirit of the Lord" (2 Corinthians 3:18).

The pursuit of purity is an ongoing process in our lives. As we draw near to God, we are transformed from glory to glory into the image of Christ. This transformation takes place through the work of the Holy Spirit in us as we surrender to Him and allow Him to purify and sanctify every aspect of our lives.

# CHAPTER 11

# TOTAL SURRENDER

*In this chapter, we will explore the theme of total surrender to God. The Bible teaches us about the importance of giving ourselves completely to Him, surrendering every area of our lives to His lordship. Through various biblical passages, we will examine the meaning of total surrender, the benefits of this surrender and how we can cultivate a life of surrender to God*

## The Call to Surrender

"I beseech you therefore, brethren, by the mercies of God, that ye present your bodies a living sacrifice, holy, acceptable unto God, which is your reasonable service" (Romans 12:1).

Paul exhorts us to present our bodies as a living sacrifice to God. This is our response to God's love and mercy. Total surrender involves turning all areas of our lives over to Him, offering ourselves completely as an act of worship.

## The Giving of the Heart

"My son, give me your heart; let your eyes observe my ways" (Proverbs 23:26).

God desires the total surrender of our heart. He invites us to trust Him, to surrender our worries, desires and longings to Him. When we surrender our hearts to God, we allow Him to guide our steps and shape our lives according to His will.

**The Surrender of the Will**

"Thy kingdom come, thy will be done, on earth as it is in heaven" (Matthew 6:10).

The Our Father's prayer teaches us to seek God's will in our lives. Total surrender involves aligning our will with God's, seeking His direction in every decision and choice we make. It is an acknowledgment that God knows what is best for us and that we are willing to follow His plan.

**The Surrender of Dreams and Plans**

"The heart of man plans his way, but the Lord directs his steps" (Proverbs 16:9).

When we surrender to God, we also surrender our dreams and plans to Him. This doesn't mean that we don't have dreams or goals, but that we are willing to allow God to direct and shape them according to His will. Total surrender involves trusting that God has the best for us and that He will guide us every step of the way.

## The Surrender of Relationships

"Love one another with brotherly love, in honor preferring one another" (Romans 12:10).

Total surrender is also reflected in our relationships. We are to love one another sincerely, humbly, and unselfishly. This involves putting the needs of others above our own, seeking reconciliation, and forgiving those who have hurt us. The surrender of relationships allows us to live in harmony and unity, reflecting God's love.

## The Surrender of Talents and Resources

"Each one should administer the gift to others as he has received it, as good stewards of the manifold grace of God" (1 Peter 4:10).

When we surrender to God, we also place our talents and resources at the service of His kingdom. He has given us unique abilities and resources to use for His glory. Total surrender involves using these gifts for the benefit of others and for the advancement of God's purpose on earth.

**Surrender as a Lifestyle**

"And he died for all, that those who live should no longer live for themselves, but for him who died for them and was raised" (2 Corinthians 5:15).

Total surrender is a way of life. It means that we no longer live for ourselves, but for God. Every aspect of our lives is surrendered to Him, seeking to please and glorify Him in all that we do. It is an ongoing journey of trust, obedience and dependence on God.

**CHAPTER 12**

# THE PATH OF RENEWAL

*In this chapter, we will explore the theme of spiritual renewal. The Bible teaches us about the importance of being renewed by God in our mind, heart and spirit. Through various biblical passages, we will examine the meaning of renewal, the benefits of this process and how we can pursue a renewed life in Christ.*

## The Need for Renewal

"Do not be conformed to this world, but be transformed by the renewing of your mind, so that you may prove what is the good, acceptable and perfect will of God" (Romans 12:2).

Renewal is essential to the Christian life. The world we live in exerts negative influences on us, moving us away from God's will. We need to be transformed by renewing our minds, allowing God to free us from the lies and patterns of the world and bring us into His perfect will.

**Mind Renewal**

"And be renewed in the spirit of your mind" (Ephesians 4:23).

Renewal begins in our mind. God calls us to renew our understanding, allowing Him to transform our thoughts and perspectives. This involves replacing lies and negative thoughts with God's truth, filling our minds with His Word and seeking a deeper understanding of who He is.

Renewal also involves the heart. We need to seek the purification of our heart before God, allowing Him to remove all impurity and restore our spirit. This implies sincere repentance, a desire to pursue holiness, and a total surrender to God.

**Renewal of the Spirit**

"Therefore we do not give up, but even if our outer man is corrupting, yet our inner man is renewed day by day" (2 Corinthians 4:16).

Renewal also affects our inner spirit. Even though we face external challenges and our bodies deteriorate over time, our spirits are renewed daily by the power of the Holy Spirit. He enables us to overcome difficulties and grow spiritually,

strengthening us to live a life of faith and
obedience.

**Renewal by the Word of God**

"Now the God of all grace, who called you to his
eternal glory in Christ Jesus, after you have
suffered a little while, he himself will perfect,
establish, strengthen, and establish you" (1 Peter
5:10).

God's Word plays a key role in spiritual renewal. It
teaches us, corrects us, encourages us, and directs
us toward righteous living. As we meditate and
apply the Word of God in our lives, we are
transformed and renewed in Christ.

**The Renewal by the Holy Spirit**

"Not by might nor by power, but by my Spirit, says the Lord of hosts" (Zechariah 4:6b).

Spiritual renewal is accomplished by the power of the Holy Spirit in us. He is the agent of transformation in our lives, enabling us to live according to God's will. We need to depend on the Holy Spirit, seeking His guidance and allowing Him to renew and empower every aspect of our lives.

## The Continuous Renewal

"So we do not lose heart; on the contrary, even if our outer man is corrupting, yet our inner man is renewed day by day" (2 Corinthians 4:16).

Spiritual renewal is an ongoing process. It's not something that happens just once, but requires a daily commitment to seek God, submit to His will and allow Him to transform us. As we surrender to

Him, our inner man is renewed day by day in the image of Christ.

**CHAPTER 13**

# REDEMPTION THROUGH HUMILITY

*In this chapter, we will explore the theme of redemption through humility. The Bible teaches us about the importance of cultivating a humble heart and how humility leads to redemption and a restored relationship with God. Through various biblical passages, we will examine the meaning of humility, the benefits of this virtue and how we can cultivate it in our lives.*

**The Importance of Humility**

"Before, what is sublime for man is lowliness of mind" (Proverbs 29:23a).

Humility is highly valued in the Word of God. It is considered a noble virtue and essential to our relationship with God and others. Humility enables us to recognize our dependence on God and to put Him first in our lives.

**The Example of Jesus**

"Have this mind in you, which was also in Christ Jesus, who, existing in the form of God, did not consider equality with God a thing to be grasped, but made himself of no reputation, taking the form of a servant, being made in the likeness of men; and being found in fashion as a man, he humbled himself, becoming obedient to death, even the death of a cross" (Philippians 2:5-8).

Jesus is the greatest example of humility. He, being God, humbled Himself by taking on human form and submitting to the Father's will, even to the point of dying on the cross for our sins. Jesus' humility teaches us to put others first and to live a life of service and sacrifice.

**The Need to Recognize Our Dependence on God**

"The Lord indeed sets a safe course for the humble, but humbles them in what is evil" (Job 22:29).

Humility leads us to recognize our total dependence on God. When we humble ourselves before Him, He directs us and guides us in safe paths. Humility helps us to let go of pride and trust God fully, recognizing that without Him we are incapable of doing anything meaningful.

**Humility in Relationships**

"With all lowliness and meekness, with longsuffering, bearing with one another in love" (Ephesians 4:2).

Humility is also fundamental to our relationships with others. It enables us to treat others with respect, patience, and love. By being humble, we are able to forgive, serve and submit to others, cultivating healthy and harmonious relationships.

**Humility as a Source of Wisdom**

"Who is wise and understanding among you? Show by your good dealings and your works in the meekness of wisdom" (James 3:13).

Humility is intrinsically linked to wisdom. Those who are humble are able to recognize their limits and seek God's guidance. Humility allows us to learn from others, accept advice and grow in wisdom.

**Humility as a Means of Seeking God's Grace**

"God opposes the proud, but gives grace to the humble" (James 4:6b).

God is pleased with those who are humble in heart. Humility opens the door to God's grace and mercy. When we recognize our need for Him and humble ourselves before Him, He extends His grace and fills us with His love and forgiveness.

**Humility as a Path to Exaltation**

"Humble yourselves, therefore, under the mighty hand of God, that he may exalt you in due time" (1 Peter 5:6).

The Bible teaches us that those who humble themselves will be exalted by God. When we submit to His will and humbly surrender, He lifts us up and honors us in His time. Humility allows us to trust in God's sovereignty and hope in His faithfulness.

# CHAPTER 14

# THE IMPORTANCE OF SERVICE

*In this chapter, we will explore the theme of the importance of servitude. The Bible teaches us about the need to be servants to one another, following the example of Jesus Christ. Through various biblical passages, we will examine the meaning of servanthood, the benefits of this posture and how we can live a life of service to others.*

**Jesus' Example of Service**

"For the Son of Man did not come to be served, but to serve and to give his life as a ransom for many" (Mark 10:45).

Jesus is the greatest example of servanthood. He came into the world not to be served, but to serve and to give His life in sacrifice for others. He washed the disciples' feet, healed the sick, fed the hungry, and taught the importance of humble service.

**The Call to Servitude**

"For you, brethren, were called to freedom. So do not use your freedom as an opportunity for the flesh, but serve one another in love" (Galatians 5:13).

As followers of Jesus, we are called to mutual servitude. The freedom we have in Christ is not to be used to satisfy our own selfish desires, but to serve one another through love. Servanthood is a practical expression of the love we show to others.

**Servitude as a Demonstration of Love**

"Love does no harm to a neighbor. So love is the fulfillment of the law" (Romans 13:10).

Serving one another is a practical expression of love. When we serve, we place the needs of others above our own, showing care, compassion, and kindness. Through servanthood, we fulfill the law of love and reflect the character of Christ in our lives.

## Servitude as Humility

"If anyone wants to be first, he will be last of all and servant of all" (Mark 9:35).

Servitude is intimately connected with humility. Those who would be great in the kingdom of God must be the servants of all. Servanthood requires putting others first, recognizing our own need for help, and valuing the dignity and well-being of others.

## The Volunteer Service

"Each one should administer the gift to others as he has received it, as good stewards of the manifold grace of God" (1 Peter 4:10).

God has given us unique gifts and talents that we are to use to serve others. As good stewards of God's grace, we should administer these gifts with generosity and joy, putting them at the service of others. Volunteer service is a practical way to express our love and gratitude to God.

**Service to the Needy**

"In everything I gave you an example that, working like this, one should help the weak, remembering the words of the Lord Jesus himself, who said: It is more blessed to give than to receive" (Acts 20:35).

Part of Christian service involves helping the needy and the weak. We must be attentive to the needs of others and offer help, comfort and support. As we serve those in need, we emulate Jesus' example and experience the joy and satisfaction that come from giving to others.

## The Reward of Servitude

"Whoever wants to be great among you must be your servant, and whoever wants to be first among you must be your servant, just as the Son of Man did not come to be served but to serve, and to give his life as a ransom for many" (Matthew 20:26-28).

While servanthood involves putting others first, God promises to reward those who serve with a sincere heart. Those who seek to be servants will be exalted by God and find true greatness in the kingdom of heaven. The eternal reward is greater than any earthly recognition or reward we can receive.

# CHAPTER 15

# THE GREATNESS OF DIVINE LOVE

*In this chapter, we will explore the theme of the greatness of divine love. The Bible reveals to us God's unconditional love for us and teaches us about the importance of loving God and others. Through various biblical passages, we will examine the meaning and magnitude of divine love, the benefits of that love and how we can live a life guided by love.*

## God's Love Revealed

"For God so loved the world, that he gave his only begotten Son, that whosoever believeth in him should not perish, but have everlasting life" (John 3:16).

Divine love is supremely revealed in the sacrifice of Jesus Christ on the cross. God loved the world so deeply and completely that He sent His only Son to die for us, that we might have eternal life. God's love is unconditional, generous and redemptive.

## The Commandment of Love

"Jesus answered him, Thou shalt love the Lord thy God with all thy heart, and with all thy soul, and with all thy mind. This is the great and first commandment.

Jesus taught us that the greatest commandment is to love God with all our being and to love our neighbor as ourselves. Love is central to the Christian life and should be the motivation behind everything we do. Love for God and others is the fulfillment of the whole law.

## The Example of Brotherly Love

"By this we know love, that Christ laid down his life for us; and we ought to lay down our lives for the brethren. Now he that hath this world's goods, and seeth his brother in need, and closeeth his heart against him, how can the love of God abide in him?" (1 John 3:16-17).

The supreme example of love is seen in the giving of Jesus for us. As followers of Christ, we are called to love one another sacrificially. This means being willing to lay down our lives for the brethren, sharing with those in need, and showing compassion and care for one another.

## The Transforming Power of Love

"To which Jesus answered, Thou shalt love the Lord thy God with all thy heart, and with all thy soul, and with all thy mind. This is the great and first commandment.

Love has the power to transform lives. When we love God with our whole being and love our neighbor as ourselves, we experience an inner transformation. God's love enables us to forgive, reconcile, show grace, and live a life of compassion and kin

## The Supremacy of Love

"Above all, however, put on love, which is the perfect link" (Colossians 3:14).

Love is the supreme virtue that must permeate all areas of our lives. It unites all other virtues and is the perfect bond that holds us together as the body of Christ. Love enables us to live in harmony, overcome differences, and show the character of Christ to the world.

## The Love That Conquers Fear

"There is no fear in love; on the contrary, perfect love casts out fear, because fear involves punishment; and he who fears is not perfected in love" (1 John 4:18).

Divine love is a love that conquers fear. When we experience God's perfect love, we are freed from fear and anxiety. Love gives us confidence and security because we know we are loved and cared for by our heavenly Father.

## The Love That Lasts Forever

"And now remain faith, hope and love, these three; but the greatest of these is love" (1 Corinthians 13:13).

Love is an eternal virtue that will remain forever. When everything else passes, love will remain. It is through love that we experience communion with God and with others. It is love that unites us as a community of faith and enables us to live a life full of meaning and purpose.

# CHAPTER 16

# APPROACHING THE SANCTIFIED FEET

*In this chapter, we will explore the theme of approaching the sanctified feet of Jesus. The Bible teaches us about the importance of surrendering before the holiness of God and approaching Him with reverence and adoration. Through various biblical passages, we will examine the spiritual significance of Jesus' feet, the examples of people who approached his feet and how we can have an attitude of humility and worship before Him.*

**The Holiness of the Feet of Jesus**

"The place you walk on is holy ground" (Exodus 3:5b).

In the Bible, Jesus' feet are considered holy. When Moses met God at the burning bush, he was told to take off his sandals because the place where he was standing was holy. In the same way, when we approach the feet of Jesus, we are approaching something sacred and worthy of reverence.

**Prayer and Adoration at the Feet of Jesus**

"While he was at table in Bethany, in the house of Simon the leper, a woman came with an alabaster box of the most precious perfume of pure nard, and breaking the alabaster box, she poured the ointment on Jesus' head" (Mark 14:3).

One of the ways we approach the sanctified feet of Jesus is through prayer and worship. In the account in Mark, a woman pours precious perfume over Jesus' head as an expression of love and adoration. This attitude demonstrates humility, devotion and total delivery before Him.

**The Washing of Feet by Jesus**

"He got up from supper, took off his outer garment, and took a towel, girded himself with it. Then he poured water into a basin and began to wash the disciples' feet and to wipe them with the towel with which he was girded" (John 13:4-5).

Another significant example is when Jesus washes His disciples' feet during the Last Supper. This attitude of humility and service demonstrates Jesus' love and willingness to serve and care for His followers. We approach the feet of Jesus when we allow Him to wash and purify us, surrendering to His will and accepting His care in our lives.

**The Kiss on the Feet of Jesus**

"Behold, a woman in the city was a sinner; and when she heard that he was at table in the Pharisee's house, she took an alabaster box of ointment; and standing behind his feet, weeping, she wet them with her tears, and wiped them with her hair, and kissed his feet, and anointed them with the ointment" (Luke 7:37-38).

Another powerful example is the account of the sinful woman who washed Jesus' feet with her tears, wiped them with her hair, and anointed them with ointment. This gesture demonstrates repentance, adoration, and gratitude. We come close to Jesus' feet when we surrender before Him, acknowledging our sinful condition and seeking His mercy and forgiveness.

## The Importance of Humility and Repentance

"Therefore, putting away all impurity and accumulation of evil, receive with meekness the implanted word, which is able to save your souls" (James 1:21).

To approach the sanctified feet of Jesus, it is necessary to have a posture of humility and repentance. We need to reject impurity and evil in our lives, receiving the Word of God with meekness. Humility leads us to recognize our need for redemption and to come to Jesus with a broken and contrite heart.

## Approaching the Feet of Jesus in Spirit and Truth

"But the hour is coming, and now is, when the true worshipers will worship the Father in spirit and in truth, for these are the ones the Father is looking for to worship" (John 4:23).

Our relationship with God is based on worshiping in spirit and in truth. Approaching the feet of Jesus involves sincere and genuine worship, in which we surrender to Him with our whole being. True worship is an act of devotion, submission, and total surrender.

## Approaching the Feet of Jesus in Eternity

"I also saw thrones on which those who were given authority to judge sat. I saw the souls of those who had been beheaded for the testimony of Jesus, and for the word of God, as many as had not worshiped the beast, nor his image, and had not received his mark on their foreheads and in their hands; and they lived and reigned with Christ a thousand years" (Revelation 20:4).

Coming close to the feet of Jesus is not just limited to this earthly life. The Bible tells us of the promise to reign with Christ for all eternity. Those who remain faithful to Jesus and worship Him, even facing persecution and trials, will be rewarded with eternal fellowship with Him.

# CHAPTER 17

# THE POWER OF DEVOTION

*In this chapter, we will explore the theme of the power of devotion. Devotion is a deep expression of love, dedication and commitment to God. The Bible teaches us about the importance of devotion in our relationship with God and how it can impact all areas of our lives. Through various biblical passages, we will examine the meaning of devotion, the benefits of this practice and how we can cultivate a fervent devotional life.*

## The Call to Devotion

"Choose life, that you and your descendants may live, by loving the LORD your God, obeying his voice, and holding fast to him; for he is your life" (Deuteronomy 30:19-20a).

Since ancient times, God has been calling His people to devotion. He invites us to love Him, hear His voice, and draw close to Him. Devotion is not just a religious practice, but a lifestyle that leads us to an intimate and profound communion with our Creator.

## Devotion as a Priority

"You will seek me and find me when you seek me with all your heart" (Jeremiah 29:13).

God wants us to seek Him with all our hearts. Devotion requires commitment and priority in our lives. It's when we put God first, dedicating time and energy to being with Him, knowing His Word and seeking His presence. Devotion requires effort and intentionality.

## Daniel's Example of Devotion

"And Daniel purposed in his heart that he would not defile himself with the portion of the king's delicacies, nor with the wine that he drank; therefore he asked the chief of the eunuchs to let him not defile himself" (Daniel 1:8).

Daniel is a powerful example of devotion. Even in a hostile environment, he remained faithful to God, refusing to contaminate himself with practices and foods contrary to divine principles. His devotion to God made him an influential leader and led him to experience great miracles and divine interventions.

**Devotion through Prayer**

"Pray without ceasing" (1 Thessalonians 5:17).

Prayer is a fundamental part of the devotional life. Through prayer, we communicate with God, express our desires, seek His guidance, and present our needs before Him. Constant prayer helps us maintain an intimate and active relationship with our heavenly Father.

**Devotion through the Word of God**

"But his delight is in the law of the LORD, and in his law he meditates day and night" (Psalm 1:2).

The Word of God is essential to our devotional life. Meditating on the Word, studying it and applying it in our lives helps us to better know God's will and grow spiritually. Through reading and reflecting on the Bible, God reveals His character, principles and promises to us.

## Devotion as Cultivation of the Presence of God

"You will seek me and find me when you seek me with all your heart" (Jeremiah 29:13).

When we seek God with all our hearts, we are cultivating His presence in our lives. Devotion brings us into a more intimate and personal relationship with Him. It is in this space of communion that we experience the transforming power of the divine presence.

## The Fruit of Devotion: Transformation and Fruitfulness

"Abide in me, and I in you; as the branch of itself cannot bear fruit unless it abides in the vine, so neither can you, unless you abide in me. I am the

105

vine, you are the branches; he who abides in me, and I in him, he bears much fruit; for without me you can do nothing" (John 15:4-5).

Devotion to God produces transformation in our lives. When we abide in Christ, we are strengthened and empowered by His grace. The result is a fruitful life where the character of Christ is manifested in us and we are used by God to positively impact the world around us.

**Devotion as a Witness to the World**

"Let your light so shine before men, that they may see your good works, and glorify your Father which is in heaven" (Matthew 5:16).

Our devotion to God is not only for our personal benefit, but also to be a living witness to the world. When we live a godly life, demonstrating love, kindness, and justice, we reflect the light of Christ and glorify God. Our devotion draws others to know and love God as well.

# CHAPTER 18

# TRANSFORMATION BY
# THE DIVINE TOUCH

*In this chapter, we'll explore the transformative power of divine touch. The Bible is full of accounts where God's touch brought healing, restoration, and transformation. Through various biblical passages, we will examine the spiritual meaning of the divine touch, the examples of people who were transformed by this touch, and how we can open our hearts to receive God's touch in our lives.*

## The Touch of God as a Source of Healing

"And behold, a woman who had been suffering from bleeding for twelve years, came up behind him and touched the edge of his cloak, for she said in her heart, 'If I just touch his garment, I will get well'" (Matthew 9:20-21).

A powerful example of divine touch as a source of healing is the account of the woman suffering from bleeding. She believed that if she could just touch the edge of Jesus' robe, she would be healed. Upon touching Jesus, she immediately received the healing she was looking for. This episode teaches us that God's touch has the power to bring physical, emotional, and spiritual healing into our lives.

**The Touch of Jesus as a Sign of Mercy**

"Now when Jesus went ashore, he saw a large crowd, and he had compassion on them and healed their sick" (Matthew 14:14).

Jesus is known for His touch of compassion and mercy. He healed the sick, restored lepers, gave sight to the blind and ears to the deaf. His touch was a sign of God's love and compassion for those in need. He cared about people's suffering and used His touch to bring relief and transformation.

**The Touch That Restores Life**

"And, approaching, he touched the bier (and those who carried it stopped), and said: Young man, I say to you, get up!" (Luke 7:14).

Jesus also demonstrated the power of His touch by raising the widow of Nain's son from the dead. He touched the bier where the body was being carried and told the dead youth to get up. Jesus' touch brought life where there was death, restoring hope and joy to that family. This episode shows us that God's touch can bring life and restoration even in the most desperate situations.

**The Touch That Sets Free**

"And stretching out his hand, he touched him, saying, I want to, be clean! And immediately the leper was cleansed of his leprosy" (Matthew 8:3).

Jesus' touch also had the power to free those trapped by disease and oppression. He healed lepers, cast out demons, and restored dignity to those who were considered untouchable. His touch brought liberation and transformation, breaking the chains that imprisoned people.

## The Touch That Opens Spiritual Eyes

"And Jesus came and spake unto them, saying, All power in heaven and on earth has been given unto me" (Matthew 28:18).

The touch of Jesus is not just limited to the physical realm. It also has the power to open spiritual eyes and reveal divine truth. When we are touched by Jesus, we are empowered to see beyond appearances and understand the mysteries of the Kingdom of God. His touch gives us spiritual insight and helps us grow in our faith.

## The Touch of God That Changes Hearts

"And stretching out his hand, Jesus touched him, saying, I will; be clean! Immediately the leprosy left him, and he was clean" (Mark 1:41).

God's touch is not just limited to physical transformation. It also has the power to transform hearts and change lives. When we are touched by God's love, our sinful nature is purified, our hearts are transformed, and we are enabled to live in righteousness and holiness. God's touch frees us from the power of sin and enables us to live a life that glorifies Him.

**Receiving God's Touch**

"Draw close to God, and he will draw close to you" (James 4:8a).

To experience God's touch, we need to approach Him with humility and an open heart. We must seek His presence, pray, read His Word, and cultivate an intimate relationship with Him. As we surrender to Him and come close in faith, we allow

His transforming touch to work within us, bringing healing, deliverance, and renewal.

# CHAPTER 19

# EXPERIENCE OF DIVINE PRESENCE

*In this chapter, we will explore the wonderful experience of divine presence. The Bible teaches us about the importance of seeking and enjoying God's presence in our daily lives. Through various biblical passages, we will examine the spiritual meaning of the divine presence, the examples of people who have experienced this presence and how we can cultivate a life of communion and intimacy with God.*

**The Promise of God's Presence**

"Fear not, for I am with you; be not dismayed, for I am your God; I will strengthen you, I will help you, I will uphold you with my faithful right hand" (Isaiah 41:10).

Since ancient times, God has promised His presence to His children. He is the God who is with us, strengthens us, helps us and sustains us. This promise fills us with confidence and encourages us to seek and experience His presence in our lives.

**Seeking the Presence of God**

"With my soul I have desired you at night, and with my spirit that is within me I will rise early to seek you; for when your judgments are in the earth, the inhabitants of the world learn righteousness" (Isaiah 26:9).

Seeking God's presence requires a burning desire in our heart. We must yearn for His presence more than anything else and be willing to sacrifice time and effort to seek Him. It's a daily commitment to draw close to Him in prayer, worship, and study of the Word.

**God's Presence as a Refuge**

"In your presence is fullness of joy; at your right hand are pleasures forevermore" (Psalm 16:11).

God's presence is a safe refuge and a place of joy. In it, we find solace, peace and contentment. When we come to Him, we are enveloped in His love and grace, finding rest for our weary souls.

**The Experience of God's Presence**

"Then Moses said, "Please show me your glory." The LORD said to him, "I will cause all my goodness to pass before you, and I will proclaim the name of the LORD to you.

Moses had a profound experience of God's presence. He longed to see the glory of God and the Lord revealed His goodness and mercy to him. This life-changing experience strengthened Moses and enabled him to lead the people of Israel with wisdom and authority.

## The Presence of God that Guides and Protects

"And the LORD said unto him, I myself will go with thee, and give thee rest" (Exodus 33:14).

God's presence guides and protects us in all circumstances. He walks with us, guides us, and gives us rest. His presence gives us security and enables us to face life's challenges with confidence.

**The Presence of God that Transforms**

"And we all, with unveiled face, beholding, as in a mirror, the glory of the Lord, are being transformed, from glory to glory, into his own image, as by the Lord, the Spirit" (2 Corinthians 3:18).

When we come into the presence of God, we are transformed. His glory surrounds us and molds us into His image. This inner transformation empowers us to live a life that reflects God's character and love.

**Cultivating a Life of Intimacy with God**

"The LORD is good to those who wait for him, to the soul that seeks him" (Lamentations 3:25).

Cultivating a life of intimacy with God requires time, dedication and perseverance. We should seek

His presence with confident expectation, knowing that He is good and willing to reveal Himself to us. This involves times of prayer, worship, meditation on the Word and obedience to His will.

**The Presence of God that Fills Us with Joy**

"You will show me the path of life; in your presence is fullness of joy, in your right hand pleasures forevermore" (Psalm 16:11).

God's presence fills us with joy and gives us a sense of purpose and meaning. When we live in His presence, we experience true joy that goes beyond our circumstances and strengthens us in all of life's situations.

# CHAPTER 20

# THE HUMBLE CARPET - AN INVITATION TO DIVINE PROXIMITY

*In this final chapter, we will explore the theme of the humble rug as an invitation to divine closeness.*

Throughout this book, we reflect on the greatness of Jesus, the essence of holiness, the call to humility, awareness of our insignificance, acceptance of our sinful condition, approaching the presence of Jesus, the carpet metaphor, submission to divine purpose, the pursuit of purity, total surrender, the path of renewal, redemption through humility, the importance of servanthood, the greatness of divine love, approaching sanctified feet, the power of devotion, transformation by divine touch, experiencing divine presence and transformation through closeness to God. Now we come to the final chapter, where we will examine the humble rug as an invitation to divine closeness.

## Humility as an Attribute Valued by God

"First of all, the fear of the LORD is the beginning of wisdom, and knowledge of the Holy One is understanding" (Proverbs 9:10).

Humility is an attribute valued by God. The Bible teaches us that the fear of the Lord is the beginning of wisdom, and knowledge of the Holy One is prudence. When we acknowledge our dependence on God and humbly submit to Him, we open the door to experiencing His closeness and wisdom.

## The Humble Rug as a Symbol of Submission

"Submit yourselves therefore to God. Resist the devil, and he will flee from you" (James 4:7).

The humble mat symbolizes our submission to God. When we place ourselves in a position of humility before Him, acknowledging His sovereignty and authority over our lives, we are demonstrating our desire to be in His presence. Submission to God brings us closer to Him and allows us to experience His closeness and protection.

**God's Exaltation of the Humble**

"Humble yourselves, therefore, under the mighty hand of God, that he may exalt you in due time" (1 Peter 5:6).

The Bible assures us that God exalts the humble. When we humble ourselves before Him, He lifts us up and honors us at the right time. Approaching God in humility is an invitation to experience His closeness and enjoy the blessings and favor He has in store for us.

**The Example of Jesus as a Humble Mat**

"Take my yoke upon you and learn from me, for I am gentle and humble in heart, and you will find rest for your souls" (Matthew 11:29).

Jesus is the perfect example of humility. He emptied Himself of His divine glory and became a servant, even washing the feet of His disciples. He invites us to learn of Him and follow His example of humility. As we submit to Him like a humble rug, we find rest and peace for our souls.

## Divine Closeness to the Humble of Heart

"The LORD is close to the brokenhearted, and saves the brokenhearted" (Psalm 34:18).

God is close to those who are brokenhearted and humble. He sympathizes with those who are downcast and approach Him in humility. To approach God as a lowly rug is to open the way to His nearness and to experience His salvation and comfort.

## Humility as a Prerequisite for Closeness to God

"Thus says the High and Lofty, who lives forever and whose name is holy: I dwell in a high and holy place, but I also dwell with him who is contrite and lowly in spirit, to revive the spirit of the lowly and to revive the heart of the contrite" (Isaiah 57:15). God dwells in a high and holy place, but he also dwells with the humble in spirit. He approaches those who have a humble and contrite heart. Humility is a prerequisite for experiencing His closeness and receiving the new life and encouragement He wants to give us.

**The Call to Continuous Humility**

"Before, he emptied himself, taking the form of a servant, becoming similar to men; and, recognized in human form, humbled himself, becoming obedient to death, even death on a cross" (Philippians 2:7-8).

The call to humility is ongoing in our spiritual journey. Just as Jesus emptied Himself of His glory and humbled Himself to death on the cross, we are called to follow His example and humble ourselves before God and others. Continuous humility is a constant invitation to divine closeness and conformity to the image of Christ.

**Living as Humble Rugs**

"If anyone wants to be first, he will be last and servant of all" (Mark 9:35).

To live as humble rugs is to embrace the call to be servants of all. It is putting the interests of others above our own, seeking to serve and love as Jesus taught us. By living as humble rugs, we open ourselves to God's closeness and become instruments of His grace and love to those around us.

## Afterword

*At the end of this journey, I am deeply grateful and moved that we have walked through the pages of this book together. The theme of the magnificence of Jesus and the search for divine closeness are extremely important in our spiritual journey.*

*Throughout the writing of this book, my desire has been to convey the greatness of our Savior and to encourage every reader to draw near to the sanctified feet of Jesus, becoming a "humble rug" before Him. Through humility, acceptance of our sinful condition and pursuit of purity, we can experience the transformation and redemption that we only find in His presence.*

*I hope that every word written here has touched your hearts, dear readers, and that you have been inspired to seek a deeper life of communion with God. Approaching the Creator is an invitation to experience the fullness of His love and mercy, finding rest and joy for our souls.*

*I want to express my gratitude to everyone who made this book possible. To God, our heavenly Father, thank you for His guidance and divine inspiration in every written word. To my family, friends, and colleagues, I am grateful for their unwavering support and constant encouragement throughout this journey.*

*To the readers, I want to thank you for dedicating your time and attention to this work. My prayer is that you will be able to apply the principles presented here in your daily lives, finding a deeper and more meaningful closeness with God.*

*May the message of this book be like a seed planted in your hearts, growing and blossoming into fruits of humility, love and service to others. May each reader be a reflection of the magnificence of Jesus in everything they do, being lights that shine in this dark world.*

*Finally, let me be sure that this journey does not end here. May each of us continue to seek the divine presence in all aspects of our lives, living as "humble rugs" that invite others to draw closer to the Savior.*

*May God bless you all with His grace and peace, and may His divine nearness be a constant reality in our spiritual journeys.*

## Author's Note

Dear readers,

*It is with immense joy and gratitude that I share with you this work that was born from a profound calling. As an independent author, every word on these pages has been inspired by the Holy Spirit, guiding me at every step of creating this book.*

*This is an initial step in my literary journey, and although resources are limited, the desire to convey the message within this book is immense. I acknowledge that the journey is filled with learning and growth, and I am aware that errors may have found their way into these pages, whether in the form of grammar or other aspects.*

*This is where I ask you, dear reader, for your valuable collaboration. If you detect any mistakes, please assist me in the pursuit of excellence. Your contribution is essential to enhance this work, making it as accurate and meaningful as possible. Please feel free to get in touch through the following email: **domingosaiolfe@gmail.com.***

*May these words touch your soul and offer insights, inspiration, and profound reflections. I thank you for embarking on this journey with me, and I hope this is only the beginning of our connection through the written word.*

*With gratitude and blessings,*

*Domingos Aiolfe*

*(Independent Author)*

# Bibliography

During the writing of this book, a variety of reference sources were used, including books, articles, academic studies, and online sources. Below, I present the bibliography that contributed to the construction of this work:

1. Bíblia Sagrada: As passagens bíblicas citadas neste livro foram retiradas de diversas versões da Bíblia, incluindo a Almeida Revista e Atualizada (ARA), a Nova Versão Internacional (NVI) e a Almeida Corrigida Fiel (ACF).

2. C. S. Lewis. "Cristianismo Puro e Simples". Editora WMF Martins Fontes, 2017.

3. John Stott. "A Mensagem do Sermão do Monte". Editora ABU, 2013.

4. Timothy Keller. "A Cruz do Rei". Editora Vida Nova, 2012.

5. Max Lucado. "Deus Está Com Você Todos os Dias". Editora Thomas Nelson Brasil, 2015.

6. Eugene Peterson. "A Mensagem". Editora Vida, 2003.

7. John MacArthur. "A Humildade". Editora Fiel, 2012.

8. John Piper. "O Supremo Valor de Conhecer a Cristo". Editora Fiel, 2010.

9. Andrew Murray. "Humildade - A Beleza da Santidade". Editora Mundo Cristão, 2015.

10. R. C. Sproul. "O Caráter de Deus". Editora Cultura Cristã, 2006.

11. Wayne Grudem. "Teologia Sistemática". Editora Vida Nova, 1999.

12. Augustus Nicodemus Lopes. "Teologia Sistemática: Uma Análise Histórica, Bíblica e Aplicada". Editora Hagnos, 2007.

13. Warren W. Wiersbe. "Comentário Bíblico Expositivo - Novo Testamento". Editora Geográfica, 2006.

14. John F. MacArthur Jr. "Comentário Bíblico MacArthur - Novo Testamento". Editora Thomas Nelson Brasil, 2008.

15. William Barclay. "Comentário Bíblico: Novo Testamento". Editora Hagnos, 2004.

16. Academic studies and theological articles that support some concepts and approaches present in this book.

17. Research online sources, including Bible study sites, theological articles, and other credible sources.

These works and references were fundamental for the construction of the arguments and reflections present in each chapter of this book. I am grateful to all the authors and scholars who, through their work, have contributed to enriching this work and making it a reliable and uplifting resource.

**END**

Printed in Great Britain
by Amazon

35916552R00079